native explore

NativeNorthwest.com • Vancouver, Canada • 604-266-9044 • info@nativenorthwest.com

Printed in Hong Kong on 50% post-consumer waste & chlorine-free paper,
using soy-based inks and non-toxic coatings.

ISBN 978-1-55471-876-4 • Second printing, February 2014
Book Design by Kylie Ward

Partial proceeds from this publication support Aboriginal learning programs.

SHARING OUR WORLD

Animals of the Native Northwest Coast

Our **ANCESTORS** lived in harmony with the wildlife that surrounded them. Each animal was honoured for its gifts and special qualities.

Carved from cedar, TOTEMS tell stories of our people's relationship to animals.

The **THUNDERBIRD** is so huge it creates thunder as it flaps its wings.

The **WOLF** is a great hunter, provider and protector.

SALMON have always been our most important food source. We can protect salmon by keeping our rivers and oceans clean.

FROGS are held in high esteem by many nations along the coast. They can live on land and in the water, teaching us to adapt to different situations.

BEAVERS are known as industrious and determined, teaching us about having purpose.

OWLS are able to see clearly in the dark and are considered to be insightful and wise.

BEARS are powerful and strong, yet humble. They offer us guidance.

OTTERS like to play and enjoy the world around them, inspiring us to enjoy life too.

RAVEN is the 'Trickster', bringing the moon, sun and stars to the world. Raven teaches us to be clever and creative.

An **EAGLE** flying overhead represents good luck. If you have ever seen an eagle up close, you understand why this majestic bird is so well respected and honoured.

TURTLES teach us to have patience, to think before we talk and to plan before we act.

HUMMINGBIRDS

provide us
with the gift
of friendship.
They represent
good fortune
and peace.

The **BUTTERFLY**, although small and fragile, is an important symbol of change within ourselves and the world.

An **OCTOPUS** has the flexibility to adjust to its surroundings, inspiring us to adapt to the different situations in which we find ourselves.

As people of the coast we are deeply connected in spirit to the **WHALE**. The song of the whale is considered by some to be the voices of our ancestors.